EFFECTIVE CHILD MANAGEMENT

A Practical Guide to Raising Respectful, Confident, and Emotionally Intelligent Children Without Fear

By Pitan Adebanjo

Copyright

Table of Contents

Introduction

Raising children in today's world presents both opportunity and challenge. Parents and caregivers are tasked not only with providing basic needs but also shaping behavior, values, and emotional intelligence.

Discipline is often misunderstood as punishment. However, true discipline is about teaching, guiding, and nurturing responsible behavior. This book presents a modern, humane approach to child management—one that replaces fear with understanding and control with guidance.

By adopting these strategies, caregivers can raise children who are confident, respectful, and emotionally balanced.

Discipline is not about control, it is about guidance. This book shows how to raise children with understanding, structure, and emotional intelligence instead of fear.

Chapter 1: The Child You Think You Know

Children are developing individuals. Their behavior reflects growth and learning, not defiance.

There is a moment every parent knows.

A moment when the child looks at you ;

not with innocence,

not with confusion,

but with resistance.

And something inside you tightens.

"Why are you behaving like this?"

The question comes out sharp.

Sometimes louder than intended.

The child says nothing.

Or worse; talks back.

And in that moment, it feels personal.

But here is the truth most parents are never told;

Your child is not fighting you.

 Your child is trying to understand the world; with tools they do not yet have.

The Misunderstanding at the Heart of Parenting

Many adults see children through a distorted lens.

We expect:

* Logic where there is development

* Control where there is impulse

* Obedience where there is curiosity

So when a child:

* Refuses instructions

* Repeats mistakes

* Acts impulsively

We label it; Disobedience.

But often, it is something else entirely.

Case Study 1:- The Broken Plate

It was a Sunday afternoon.

The house was quiet, unusually quiet.

Ngozi was in the kitchen when she heard it.

A sharp crash.

Glass against tile.

She rushed out.

There stood her son, Chika. Frozen.

A broken plate at his feet.

"What did you do?!" she shouted.

Silence.

"I asked you a question!"

"I… I didn't mean to," he said, his voice trembling.

The anger came instantly.

That plate was part of a set. Imported. Expensive.

Without thinking, she slapped him.

"Be careful next time!"

What Happened Next

Chika nodded.

Quiet.

Too quiet.

And from that day forward, something changed.

When he made mistakes, he hid them.

When things broke, he stayed silent.

When asked questions, he lied.

The Lesson He Learned

Not:

"Be careful"

But:

"Mistakes are dangerous. Hide them."

This Is Where Discipline Goes Wrong

Most discipline focuses on:

* The action

* The mistake

* The immediate correction

But ignores:

The lesson the child internalizes

It should be however noted that, **Children Do Not Learn What You Say.**

They learn:

* What you **'do'**

* How you **'react'**

* What your behavior **'teaches indirectly'**

Rewriting That Moment

Imagine a different response.

Same situation.

Same broken plate.

Ngozi walks in.

Sees the mess.

Sees her son.

Afraid.

She pauses.

Just for a second.

Then says:

"Are you hurt?"

He shakes his head.

She exhales.

"Okay. Come. Let's clean it together."

Later, she adds:

"Next time, be more careful. These things can break."

What Changed?

Everything.

The lesson becomes:

* Mistakes can be handled

* Truth is safe

* Responsibility is shared

* Care matters

We are not just correcting behavior.

We are shaping:

* Beliefs

* Emotional responses

* Future decision-making

As a parent , tutor or caregiver, you must be ready to make a shift which is,

Stop asking:

"How do I stop this behavior?"

Rather start asking:

"What is my child learning from this moment?"

The Reality of Child Development

Children:

* Act before thinking

* Feel before reasoning

* Learn through repetition

* Copy what they see

They are not:

* Fully logical

* Emotionally regulated

* Self-controlled

That comes later.

The Danger of Adult Expectations

When you expect adult behavior from a child:

You create:

* Frustration (in you)

* Fear (in them)

What You Must Understand

Your child is not:

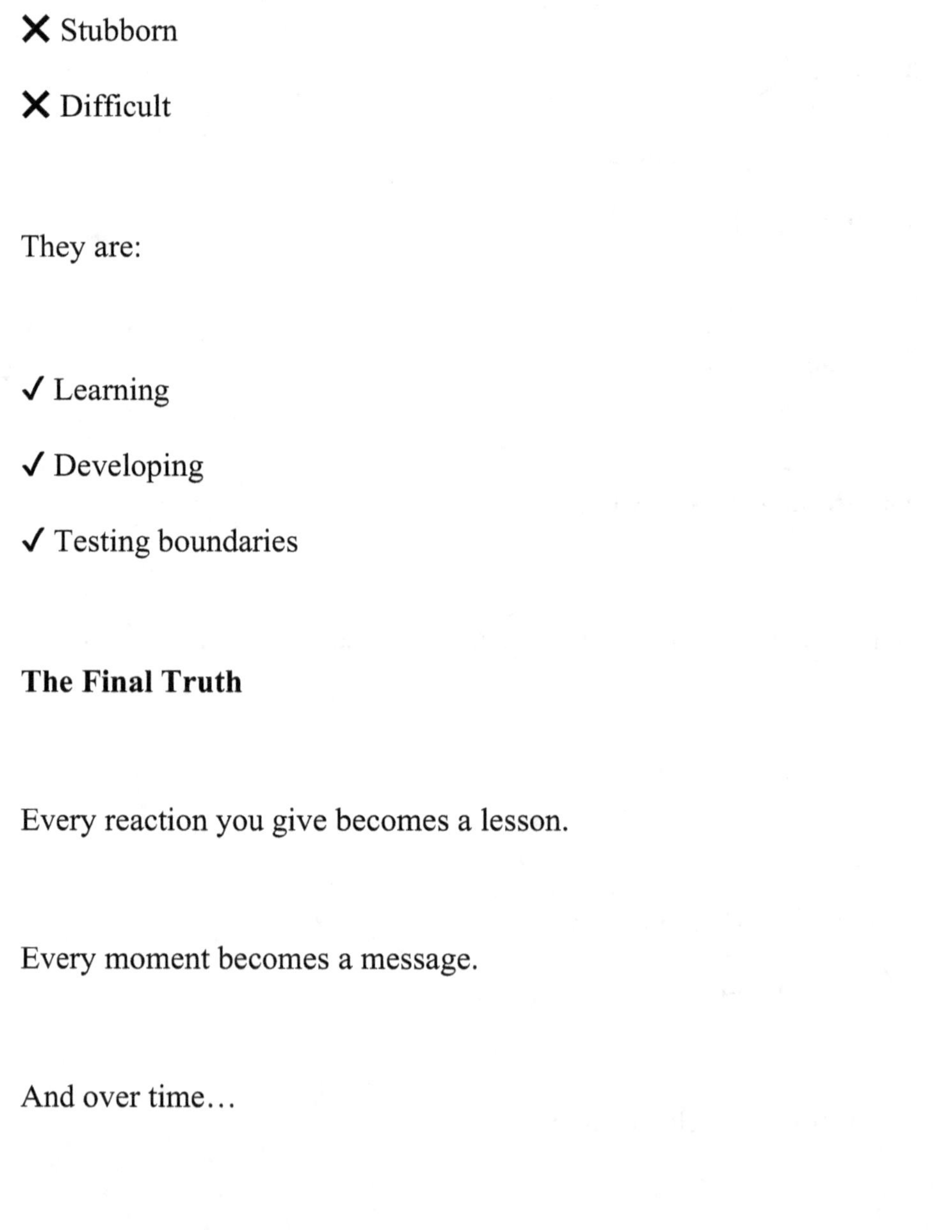

✗ Disrespectful

✗ Stubborn

✗ Difficult

They are:

✓ Learning

✓ Developing

✓ Testing boundaries

The Final Truth

Every reaction you give becomes a lesson.

Every moment becomes a message.

And over time…

Those messages become your child's inner voice.

Chapter 2: Why Corporal Punishment Fails

Fear-based discipline creates compliance but damages trust and emotional growth.

The Inheritance of Pain

There is a sentence many adults carry without questioning:

"I was beaten, and I turned out fine."

It is often said with certainty.

Sometimes even pride.

But beneath that statement is something rarely examined.

What does *"fine"* actually mean?

Does it mean:

* You never felt afraid as a child?

* You always understood why you were punished?

* You learned responsibility… or just avoidance?

Or does it simply mean:

You survived it.

Case Study1: The Boy Who Only Behaved When Watched

Maxwell was the "good child."

At least, that's what everyone said.

At home:

* He obeyed immediately

* He spoke politely

* He followed every instruction

His father believed in strict discipline.

There were rules.

And there were consequences.

Quick ones.

Firm ones.

Painful ones.

And so, Maxwell learned.

Not responsibility.

Not understanding.

But something else.

He Learned to Watch

When his father was present:

✓ Perfect behavior

When his father was absent:

✗ A different child entirely

He broke rules.
Ignored instructions.
Did what he wanted.

But carefully.

Quietly.

What Was Really Happening?

Maxwell was not disciplined.

He was **conditioned**

He did not learn:

"This is right."

He learned;

"Do not get caught."

The Hidden Cost of Fear-Based Discipline

Corporal punishment works, **temporarily**.

That's why it survives.

It produces:

* Immediate silence

* Instant compliance

But at a deeper level, it creates:

✖ Fear instead of understanding

✖ Secrecy instead of honesty

✖ Resentment instead of respect

Case Study 2: The Girl Who Became Silent

Aminat used to laugh loudly.

Too loudly, her aunt would say.

"Girls should not behave like that."

Whenever she made mistakes, the correction was swift.

A slap.

A harsh word.

A look that said: *you should know better.*

At first, she protested.

Then she explained.

Then she cried.

And then…

She stopped.

 The Transformation

Not into a "better child."

But into a quieter one.

A smaller one.

She spoke less.

Shared less.

Expressed less.

 What Changed?

Her behavior improved.

But her *voice disappeared*.

 ☐ **The Danger Nobody Talks About**

Corporal punishment doesn't always create rebellion.

Sometimes, it creates:

 Withdrawal.

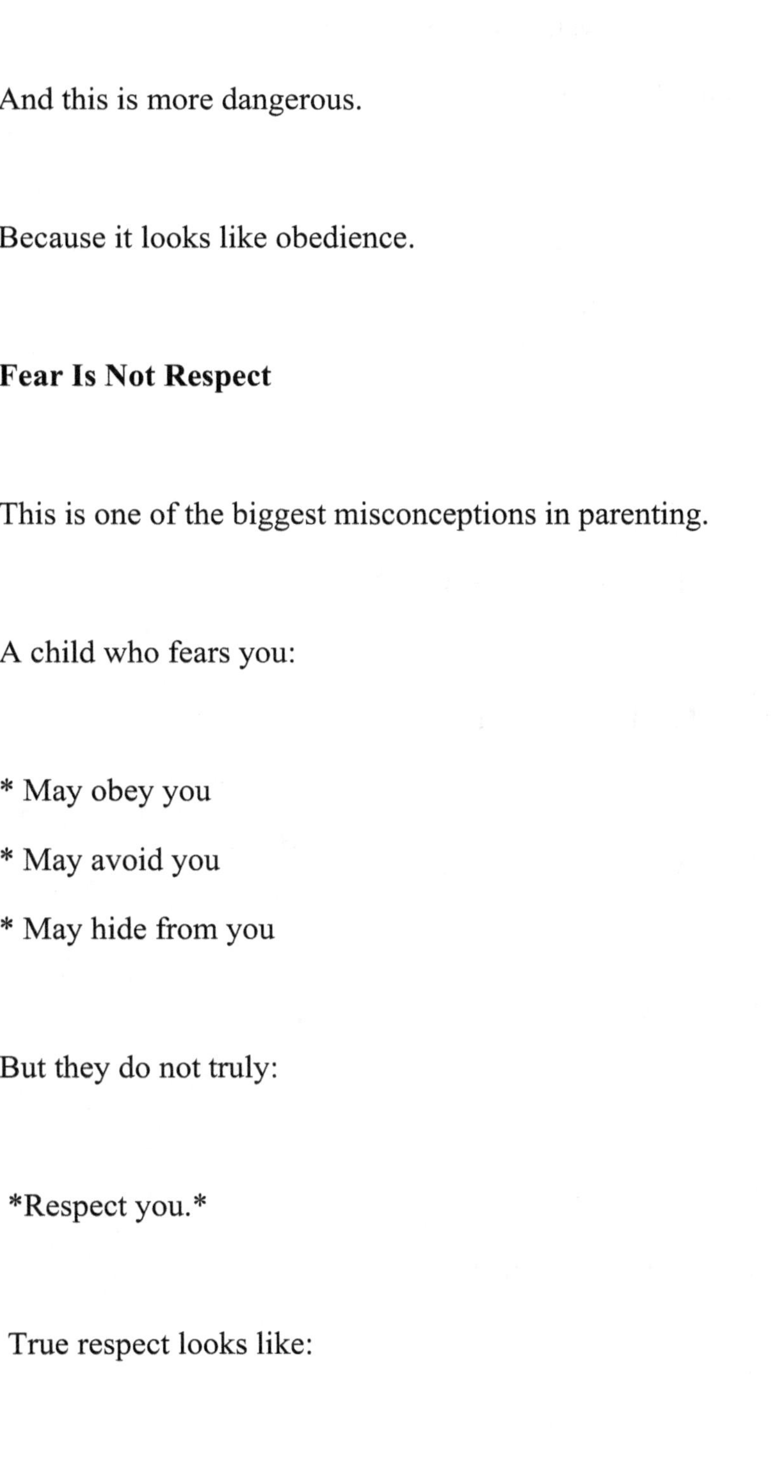

And this is more dangerous.

Because it looks like obedience.

Fear Is Not Respect

This is one of the biggest misconceptions in parenting.

A child who fears you:

* May obey you

* May avoid you

* May hide from you

But they do not truly:

Respect you.

True respect looks like:

* Doing what is right, even when you are not there

* Speaking honestly, even when afraid

* Trusting you, even after mistakes

Fear cannot produce that.

Only:

 Connection + guidance + consistency

Case Study 3: The Lie That Grew

Dan broke the window.

It was an accident.

But he ran.

When his father asked, he denied it.

Firmly.

Convincingly.

Later, the truth came out.

Punishment followed.

"Why did you lie?" his father demanded.

But the real question was:

Why did he feel he had to?

The Real Reason Children Lie

Children lie when:

* Truth feels dangerous

* Mistakes feel unforgivable

* Punishment feels certain

They are not choosing dishonesty.

They are choosing:

Safety.

A Powerful Shift,;

Instead of asking:

"How do I stop my child from lying?"

Ask:

"What makes honesty feel unsafe?"

What Corporal Punishment Actually Teaches

It teaches children:

* Avoid pain

* Hide mistakes

* Fear authority

* Obey under pressure

But it does NOT teach:

* Self-control

* Responsibility

* Emotional regulation

Moral reasoning

The Long-Term Effect

A child raised on fear may grow into an adult who:

* Struggles to express emotions

* Avoids responsibility when unsupervised

* Fears authority but does not respect it

* Repeats the same cycle

Breaking the Cycle

Many parents do not *choose* corporal punishment.

They inherit it.

It is what they know.

What they experienced.

What they were told works.

But awareness creates a choice.

And choice creates change.

A Moment of Reflection

Think about your own childhood.

Not just what you were taught.

But how you felt.

* Were you understood?

* Were you afraid?

* Did you feel safe making mistakes?

Now ask yourself:

What do I want my child to feel?

The Truth You Must Accept

If discipline is based on fear:

It will always require:

* Your presence

* Your authority

* Your control

But if discipline is based on understanding:

It creates something far more powerful:, which is, *Internal control.*

Final Truth

Corporal punishment may shape behavior.

But it does not shape character.

If your goal is not just:

A child who obeys…

But:

A human being who understands, chooses, and grows

Then the method must change.

Chapter 3: Positive Discipline in Action

Positive discipline focuses on teaching responsibility through calm, consistent guidance.

When Shouting Stops Working

Every parent reaches a moment of exhaustion.

The instructions have been repeated.

The warnings have been issued.

The threats have been made.

And still, the behavior continues.

So the voice rises.

"Didn't I tell you to stop that?!"

The child freezes.

Or worse; keeps going.

And in that moment, frustration mixes with helplessness.

Most parents believe shouting is a sign of authority.

But often, it is a sign that:

 Our methods have stopped being effective.

Case Study 1: The Morning Battle

Every morning at 6:30 a.m., the same drama unfolded in the Ferdinand household.

"Rita, wake up!"

No response.

"Rita!"

A groan from under the blanket.

"Do you want to be late again?"

Silence.

By 7:00 a.m., the house was filled with tension.

Her mother would finally pull the blanket off and shout.

"Why do you always make things difficult?"

The Pattern;

The child delayed.
The mother shouted.
The child rushed.
Everyone left the house angry.

This happened *every day*.

The Problem Was Not Laziness

When her mother finally asked calmly one evening, the truth emerged.

"I don't like school mornings," Chiamaka whispered.

"It feels too fast."

The issue was not stubbornness.

It was:

* anxiety

* overwhelm

* lack of structure

What Positive Discipline Really Means

Many people misunderstand positive discipline.

They think it means:

* no rules

* no consequences

* letting children do whatever they want

That is not discipline.

That is neglect.

Positive discipline is:

Firm. Calm. Consistent. Respectful.

It replaces:

* shouting → clarity

* punishment → consequences

* fear → understanding

Rewriting the Morning Routine

The next day, her mother tried something different.

At night, they prepared together:

* Uniform laid out

* School bag packed

* Shoes by the door

In the morning, instead of shouting, she used a calm routine:

"Chiamaka, it's time. Let's start the day."

Still sleepy, but less resistance.

Within a week, mornings became smoother.

Not perfect.

But peaceful.

Positive Discipline Works Because It Is Predictable

Children feel safer and behave better, when they know:

* What is expected

* What will happen next

* What the consequences are

Chaos creates resistance.

Structure creates cooperation.

Case Study 2 : The Homework War

Ken hated homework.

Every evening, it was a fight.

"Do your homework now!"

"I'll do it later!"

Later never came.

So punishment followed.

No TV.
No playing outside.

Still, the problem continued.

The Hidden Issue

When his mother sat beside him one day, she noticed something.

He wasn't refusing homework.

He was struggling with it.

He didn't understand the math.

Avoidance was easier than embarrassment.

Positive Discipline Starts with Curiosity

Instead of assuming; disobedience

Ask:

What is making this difficult for my child?

From Command to Collaboration

That evening, she tried a new approach.

"Let's look at this together," she said.

At first, he resisted.

Then slowly, he leaned closer.

Within minutes, he was solving problems.

Not because he was forced.

But because he felt supported.

Why Punishment Often Backfires

Punishment focuses on:

 stopping behavior

But positive discipline focuses on:

* teaching skills

A child who avoids homework does not need punishment.

They need:

* confidence

* guidance

* patience

The Core Tools of Positive Discipline

1. Clear Expectations

Children cannot follow rules they do not understand.

Instead of:

 "Behave yourself."

Say:

"We speak politely in this house."

2. Consistent Consequences

Not angry reactions, predictable outcomes.

Example:

"If toys are not packed away, they will be kept aside until tomorrow."

3. Calm Delivery

The message matters, but so does the tone.

A calm voice:

* builds authority

* reduces resistance

* keeps dignity intact

Case Study 3:- The Shop Tantrum

In a crowded Lagos market, a young boy began to scream when his mother refused to buy a toy.

Heads turned.

Whispers started.

The mother felt the familiar heat of embarrassment.

Her instinct was to slap him, to silence the noise.

Instead, she knelt beside him.

"I know you want it," she said quietly.

"But we are not buying toys today."

He cried louder, for a moment.

Then softer.

Then stopped.

What She Did Right

She:

* acknowledged his feeling
* kept her boundary

* stayed calm under pressure

That is positive discipline in action.

Why This Method Builds Stronger Children

Children raised with positive discipline develop:

* Better emotional control

* Stronger problem-solving skills

* Higher self-esteem

* Greater respect for others

Because they are taught:

* not just what to do

* but *why* it matters

What Many Parents Fear

"If I stop being strict, my child will become spoiled."

This fear is understandable.

But there is a difference between:

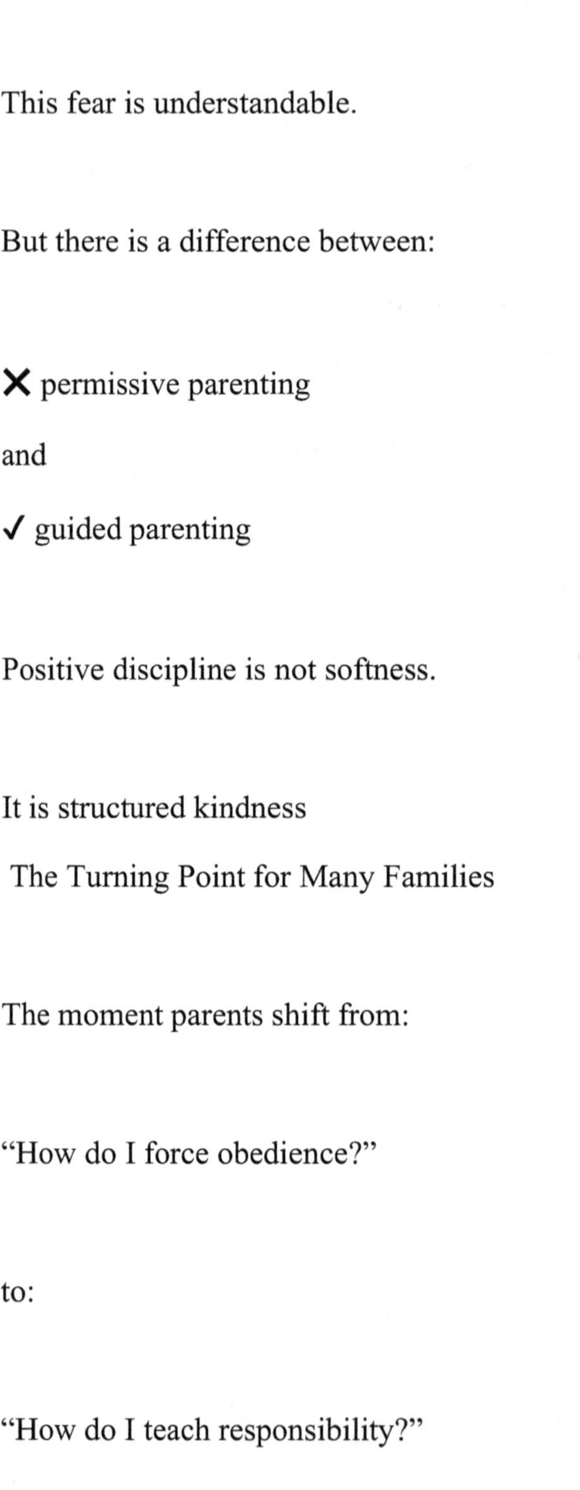

✗ permissive parenting

and

✓ guided parenting

Positive discipline is not softness.

It is structured kindness

 The Turning Point for Many Families

The moment parents shift from:

"How do I force obedience?"

to:

"How do I teach responsibility?"

Everything begins to change.

A Practical Exercise for Readers

Tonight, observe your child's behavior.

When something goes wrong, pause and ask:

* What is my child feeling?

* What skill might they be lacking?

* What lesson do I want this moment to teach?

The Long Term Goal

You are not raising a child to behave for you.

You are raising a future adult to function in society.

Punishment may control the present.

But positive discipline shapes the future.

Final Truth

A child who is guided learns to guide themselves.

And that is the true meaning of discipline.

Chapter 4: Emotional Intelligence

Children must learn to recognize, express, and regulate emotions effectively.

So Zainab tried to stop.

She held it in.

Pressed her lips together.

Fought the tears.

But the emotions didn't disappear.

They built up.

Until one day, She exploded.

What Happened?

Zainab wasn't "too emotional."

She was:

emotionally unsupported.

Suppressing Emotion Is Not Emotional Control

When children are told:

* "Stop crying"
* "Don't be angry"
* "Be strong"

They don't learn control.

They learn: *to hide.*

The Goal Is Not Less Emotion

It is:

Better expression.

The Language of Emotion

Children need help learning the words for what they feel.

Instead of:

"Stop shouting!"

Say:

"You sound frustrated."

Instead of:

"Don't cry!"

Say:

"That made you sad, didn't it?"

This does something powerful:

It gives the child:

language instead of reaction

Case Study 1: The Child Who Hit

Five-year-old Sadiq hit his younger sister whenever she touched his toys.

Every time, the reaction was immediate:

"Stop that!"

"Why are you so aggressive?"

Punishment followed.

Still, the behavior continued.

One Day, Something Changed

Instead of reacting, his mother paused.

She held his hand and said:

"You don't like it when she takes your things."

He nodded.

"You feel angry."

Another nod.

Then she added:

"You can say: 'That's mine. Please give it back.'
You don't need to hit."

What Happened Next

It didn't stop immediately.

But gradually:

The hitting reduced.

The words increased.

Why This Worked

Because the problem was not discipline.

It was, lack of emotional tools.

Emotional Skills Every Child Must Learn

1. Naming Emotions

"I am angry."
"I feel left out."
"I am scared."

2. Understanding Triggers

"What made me feel this way?"

 3. Regulating Response

"What can I do instead?"

4. Expressing Safely

"How do I say this without hurting others?"

⚠️ What Happens When This Is Not Taught

Children grow into adults who:

* React impulsively

* Struggle with relationships

* Suppress emotions until they explode

* Misinterpret others

A Powerful Parenting Shift

Instead of focusing only on behavior:

Focus on:

the emotion behind the behavior

Case Study 2 : The Quiet Child

Tessy rarely spoke.

At home, she was obedient.

Too obedient.

No complaints.

No resistance.

At first, her parents were proud.

"She's such a good child."

But her teacher noticed something different.

"She doesn't participate," she said.

"She seems afraid to speak."

The Hidden Reality

Tessy had learned:

* Mistakes lead to correction

* Expression leads to judgment

So silence felt safer.

The Lesson;

Not all well-behaved children are thriving.

Some are simply:

avoiding attention.

How to Build Emotional Intelligence at Home

1. Create Emotional Safety

Let your child know:

"You can tell me anything."

2. Listen Without Interrupting

Even when it's uncomfortable.

3. Validate First, Correct Later

Say:

"I understand why you felt that way…"

Then guide behavior.

---

4. Model It Yourself

If you:

* shout → they learn shouting

* stay calm → they learn calm

The Parent's Role

You are not just correcting actions.

You are teaching:

* how to feel

* how to respond

* how to exist in the world

A Simple Daily Practice

At the end of each day, ask your child:

* "What made you happy today?"

* "What made you upset?"

This builds:

* awareness

* communication

* connection

Final Truth

A child who understands their emotions:

* fights less

* communicates more

* grows stronger internally

And over time…

*They no longer need you to control them.

 They learn to control themselves.*

Chapter 5: Real-Life Parenting Challenges

Everyday situations provide opportunities for guidance and connection.

Where Theory Meets Reality

It is easy to talk about patience….until your child refuses to listen.

It is easy to speak about calm discipline ….until you are tired, stressed, and overwhelmed.

It is easy to promise yourself:

"I will handle things differently."

Until real life happens.

This chapter is not about perfect parenting.

It is about *real moments* messy, emotional, frustrating moments and how they can be handled differently.

Case Study 1: The Child Who Ignored You

"Come here!"

No response.

"Did you hear me?!"

Still nothing.

Your voice rises.

"I said come here NOW!"

The child finally comes, slowly, reluctantly.

Already defensive.

Already tense.

What It Feels Like

Disrespect.

Disobedience.

Defiance.

 What It Often Is

Something much simpler:

Deep focus.

Children get absorbed in:

* play

* imagination

* activity

In those moments, your voice becomes background noise.

The Shift

Instead of shouting from a distance:

Walk closer.

Lower your voice.

Make eye contact.

"Come, I need you."

Why This Works

You move from:

✘ command at a distance

to

✓ connection up close

Case Study 2: The Child Who Says "No" to Everything**

"Go and take your bath."

"No."

"Do your homework."

"No."

"Stop that."

"No."

It feels intentional.

Like the child is trying to challenge you.

The Hidden Truth

This is often a stage of development.

The child is discovering: *independence*

The word "no" becomes power.

A way of saying:

"I exist. I choose."

The Wrong Response

Force.

Threats.

Anger.

This turns a phase into a battle.

The Better Approach: Controlled Choice

Instead of:

"Go and bathe now!"

Say:

"Do you want to bathe now or in 10 minutes?"

The child still bathes.

But now feels:

included, not controlled

Case Study 3: The Child Who Embarrasses You in Public

It happens in the worst places:

* A market

* A church

* A family gathering

The child shouts.

Cries.

Refuses to cooperate.

Everyone is watching.

The Pressure

You feel judged.

Exposed.

Embarrassed.

And the instinct comes fast:

""Stop this now!"*

Sometimes with force.

But Here's the Reality

Your child is not performing for the public.

They are overwhelmed.

* Too much noise

* Too many people

* Too many emotions

The Calm Response

Instead of reacting to the crowd:

Focus on the child.

Lower yourself to their level.

Speak calmly:

"I know this is hard. Let's step outside."

What Matters Most

Not:

What people think

But:

What your child learns from the moment

Case Study 4: The Child Who Lies

"Did you break this?"

"No."

You already know the truth.

And now, you feel two things:

* Anger

* Disappointment

The Usual Reaction

Punish the lie.

Scold the child.

Demand honesty.

The Real Question

Why did the child feel unsafe telling the truth?

Most Children Lie Because:

* They fear punishment

* They want to avoid disappointment

* They feel ashamed

The Better Response

"I'm not upset about what happened.

I want us to always tell the truth."

This teaches:

✓ Honesty is safe

✓ Mistakes are allowed

✓ Trust matters

Case Study 5: The Child Who Refuses Responsibility

You ask them to clean.

They delay.

Complain.

Avoid.

Eventually, you get tired…

And do it yourself.

 What This Teaches

Not:

 Responsibility

But:

"If I wait long enough, someone else will do it."

The Solution: Follow Through

If the task is theirs—keep it theirs.

Stay calm.

Stay firm.

Stay consistent.

Case Study 6: The Sibling Conflict

"They hit me!"

"No, they started it!"

"That's not true!"

Noise. Chaos. Accusations.

The Mistake Many Parents Make

Immediately choosing sides.

Punishing quickly.

A Better Way

Pause.

Separate.

Then ask:

"What happened?"

Let each child speak.

Then guide:

"How could you handle this differently next time?"

What This Builds

* Conflict resolution

* Accountability

* Communication skills

 The Pattern Behind All These Situations

Different behaviors.

Same root:

Children struggling with skills they have not yet learned.

 The Core Skills Children Need

* Emotional control

* Communication

* Patience

* Responsibility

And discipline should focus on:

reaching these, and not punishing their absence**

A Moment of Honesty

There will be days when:

* You lose your temper

* You shout

* You react instead of respond

That does not make you a bad parent.

It makes you:

human

What Matters Most

Not perfection.

But awareness.

And willingness to improve.

Final Truth

Every difficult moment is a choice:

* React… or guide

* Control… or teach

* Punish… or build

And over time…

Those choices shape not just behavior, but **who your child becomes.***

Chapter 6: Practical Discipline for Everyday Life
Consistency and calm action build lasting discipline.

No shouting.

No drama.

Just follow through.

 4. Reward System (Used Wisely)

Not bribes.

But recognition.

 Example:

"I noticed you packed your toys without being told."

This builds:

* confidence

* repetition of good behavior

Common Mistakes to Avoid

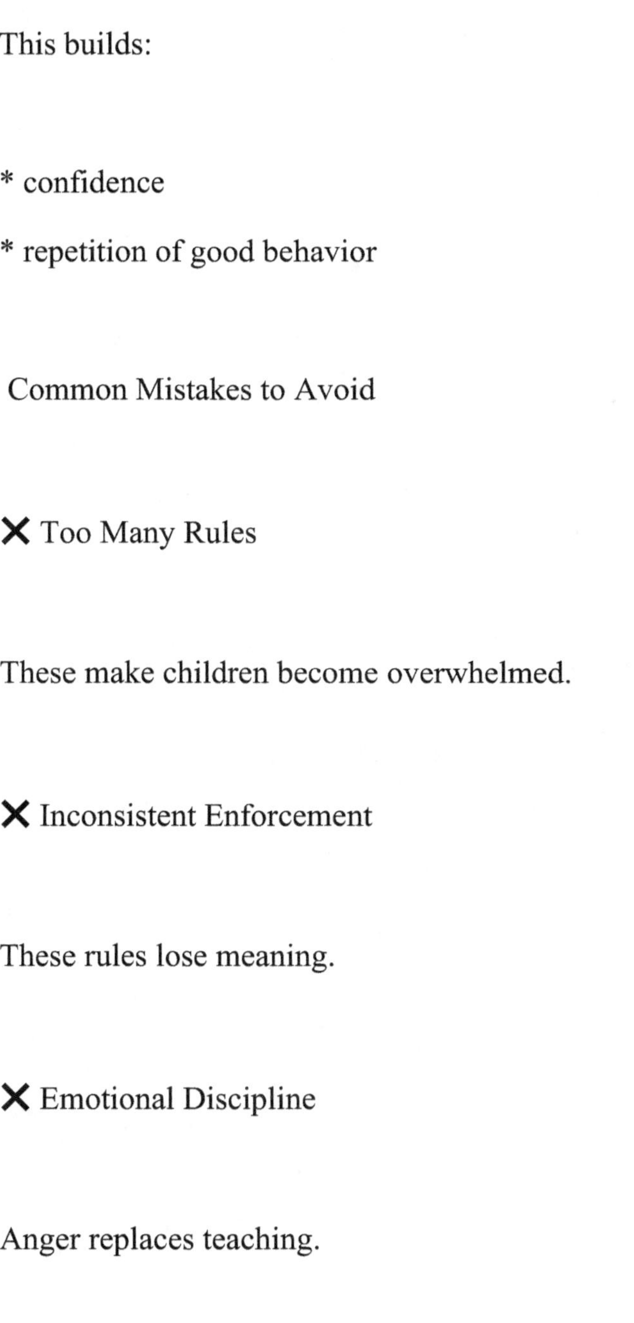

✖ Too Many Rules

These make children become overwhelmed.

✖ Inconsistent Enforcement

These rules lose meaning.

✖ Emotional Discipline

Anger replaces teaching.

✖ Expecting Instant Change

Growth takes time.

A Realistic Truth

You will repeat yourself sometimes.

You will lose patience sometimes.

You will get it wrong sometimes.

All of these are part of the process.

What Matters Most

Not perfection.

But:

progress + consistency

A Powerful Daily Habit

At the end of each day, reflect;

* What did I handle well?

* Where did I react too quickly?

* What will I do differently tomorrow?

This turns parenting into:

growth, for both you and your child

The Long Term Effect

It should be noted that children raised with consistent, calm discipline:

* Listen more

* Resist less

* Trust more

* Grow stronger internally

Final Truth

Discipline is not built in moments of anger.

It is built in moments of:

clarity, consistency, and calm action

And over time those moments shape behavior,.habits and character.

Chapter 7: Handling Difficult Behaviors

Difficult behavior signals unmet needs or undeveloped skills.

When Simple Strategies Stop Working

There are moments when nothing seems to work.

You've tried:

* explaining

* warning

* guiding

And still, the behavior continues.stronger, louder, and more resistant.

It is in these moments many parents think:

"This child is just difficult."

But here is the truth;

There is no "difficult child."

But, only a child struggling with something they cannot yet manage.

Understanding Difficult Behavior

What we call difficult behavior is often:

* unmet needs

* unexpressed emotions

* undeveloped skills

So instead of asking:

"How do I stop this?"

Ask:

"What is driving this?"

Case Study 1: The Defiant Child

"Sit down."

"No."

"Sit down now!"

"No!"

The tension rises.

It becomes a battle of authority.

What It Looks Like

Disrespect.

Stubbornness.

Defiance.

What It Often Is

A struggle for *control and autonomy*

Why Defiance Happens

Children push back when they feel:

* controlled

* unheard

* powerless

The Strategy: Reduce the Power Struggle

Instead of escalating;

Give structured control.

Example:

Instead of:

"Sit down now!"

Say:

"Would you like to sit here or there?"

Same outcome.

Less resistance.

Case Study 2: The Child Who Throws Tantrums

It starts small.

Then grows.

* crying

* shouting

* rolling on the floor

Nothing works.

The Parent Feels embarrassed, angry and overwhelmed.

What a Tantrum Really Is

Not manipulation.

Not bad behavior.

But, *emotional overload*

The child is not thinking.

They are reacting.

The required strategy to handle this concerned behavior is to stay calm, and stay close.

Do not:

✗ shout

✗ threaten

✗ punish in the moment

Instead:

* Stay near

* Stay calm

* Let the wave pass

Afterwards, teach.

Not during.

Why This Works

You cannot teach during emotional chaos

Only after emotional calm

Case Study 3: The Aggressive Child

When a child exhibits characters such as, Hitting, Pushing and Throwing things. The usual response would be;

"Stop that!"

Punishment.

Anger.

 The aftermath of the above reaction will be;

Aggression continues.

The Root of Aggression

Often:

* frustration

* inability to express

* modeled behavior

Expected strategy to use is to replace the Behavior.

Don't just say:

"Don't hit."

Teach what to do instead

Example:

"You're angry.

Use your words."

Or:

"Step away.

Take a breath."

Note that *Behavior Must Be Replaced, Not Just Removed*

If you remove a behavior without replacing it:

It returns.

Case Study 4: The Child Who Withdraws

Not loud.

Not disruptive.

But distant.

They:

* avoid conversation

* stay quiet

* disconnect

The Hidden Risk

This behavior is often ignored.

Because it is not "troublesome."

 What Withdrawal Means

The child may feel:

* unsafe

* unheard

* emotionally shut down

The Strategy: Rebuild Connection

Not pressure.

Not interrogation.

But:

* gentle conversation

* shared time

* emotional safety

Case Study 5: The Repeating Behavior

You correct it.

It stops.

Then returns.

Again.

And again.

The Parent's Thought

"Why don't they learn?!"

The Truth

Children learn through:

repetition

Not one-time correction.

The Strategy: Consistent Reinforcement

Same message.

Same response.

Repeated calmly.

The Biggest Mistake in Difficult Situations

Reacting emotionally is a great mistake to be allowed.

 When emotion leads:

* voice rises

* clarity drops

* learning stops

The Golden Rule

Calm is your greatest authority

 It should be however noted that what difficult behavior Is really asking are as follows;

* "Do you understand me?"

* "Am I safe?"

* "Do I have control?"

* "Will you guide me or fight me?"

 Your role in these moments is;

Not to *win.*

But to *lead*

A Real Parenting Truth

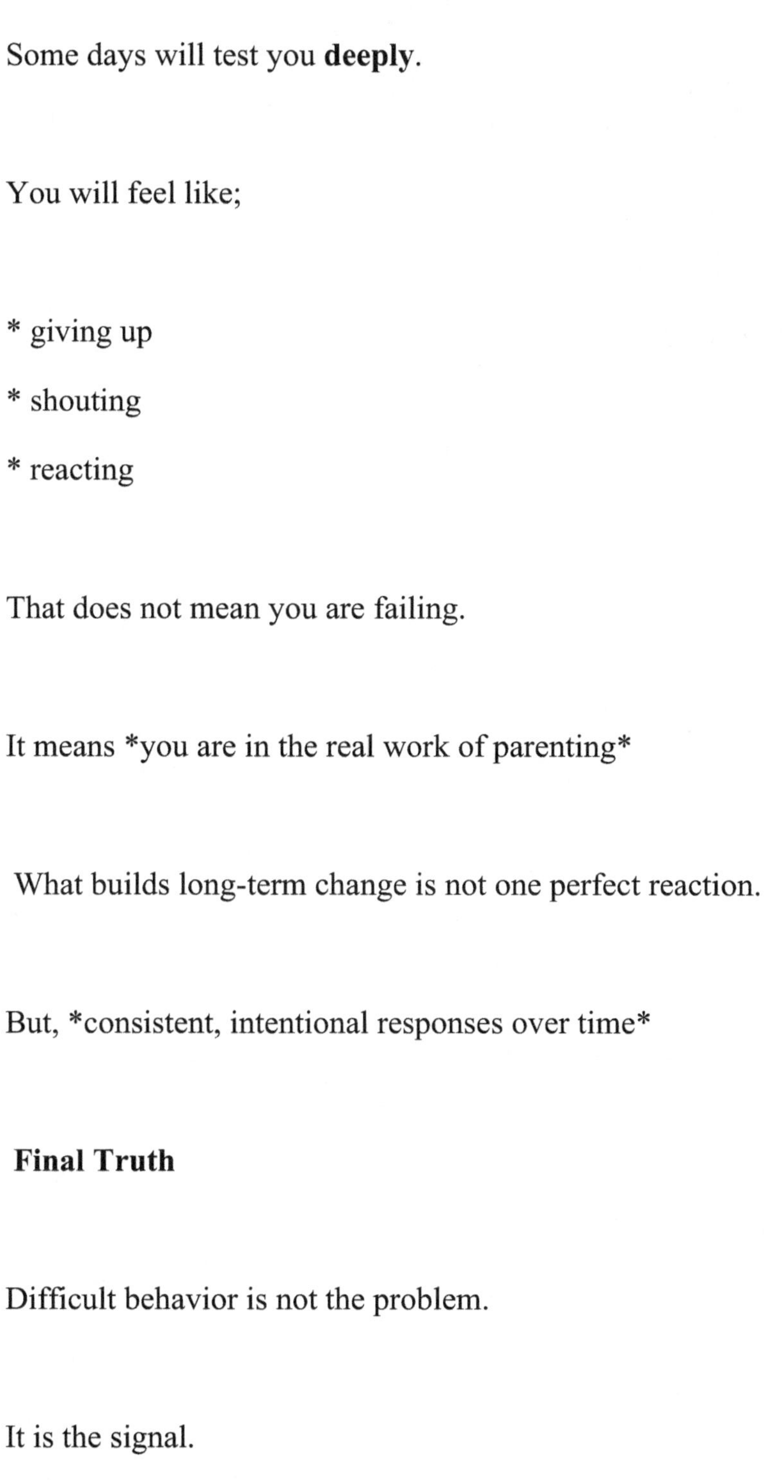

Some days will test you **deeply**.

You will feel like;

* giving up

* shouting

* reacting

That does not mean you are failing.

It means *you are in the real work of parenting*

 What builds long-term change is not one perfect reaction.

But, *consistent, intentional responses over time*

Final Truth

Difficult behavior is not the problem.

It is the signal.

When you learn to read it correctly…

* You stop fighting your child

* And start guiding them.

Chapter 8: Communication and Trust

Trust and communication strengthen discipline and cooperation.

The Conversation That Never Happened

"Why didn't you tell me?"

The question came too late.

The damage had already been done.

The mistake had already grown.

The silence had already settled.

The child stood there, quiet, guarded.

"I didn't think you would understand," they said.

And in that moment, the parent realized something painful:

The problem was not just the behavior. It was the absence of trust.

The Invisible Gap

Many families function with rules, structure, and discipline.

But beneath all that, there is often a gap.

A silent one.

Children:

* obey

* respond

* follow instructions

But they do not:

open up

They don't share:

* fears

* mistakes

* confusion

Because somewhere along the way, they learned;

"It's safer to stay quiet."

Obedience Without Trust Is Fragile

A child may listen to you…

But still not feel safe with you.

They may;

* follow rules

* behave properly

But when it truly matters;

They won't come to you.

And that is where real problems begin.

Case Study 1 : The Hidden Problem

Fifteen-year-old Dan had been struggling in school.

His grades dropped.

His behavior changed.

He became distant.

His father responded the only way he knew how:

"Why are your results like this?"

"You need to do better!"

"Focus!"

Dan nodded.

Said nothing.

But the truth was this,

He didn't understand the subjects anymore.

He was confused.

Embarrassed.

Overwhelmed.

And he said nothing.

Why?

Because every conversation felt like:

correction not connection

The Core Truth

Children speak more when they feel;

* safe

* heard

* understood

Not when they feel;

* judged

* rushed

* dismissed

Communication Is More Than Talking

Many parents believe communication means giving instructions

But real communication is; exchange.

Not talking *at* your child

But, talking *with* them

The Two Types of Communication

✕ Directive Communication

"Do this."

"Stop that."

"Why did you do that?"

✓☐ Connective Communication

"How are you feeling?"

"What happened?"

"Help me understand."

Which Type of Communication Builds Trust?

Always *connection before correction*

Case Study 2 :The Child Who Finally Spoke

For years, Musa barely shared anything.

Short answers.

Avoided conversations.

His mother decided to try something different.

No lectures.

No corrections.

Just presence.

One evening, she sat beside him and asked:

"What was the hardest part of your day?"

He shrugged.

Silence.

She didn't push.

Just stayed.

A few minutes later, he spoke.

Slowly.

Carefully.

And for the first time in a long time, he opened up.

 What Changed?

Not the child but, the environment.

Trust Is Built in Small Moments

Not big speeches.

Not serious lectures.

But through;

* daily conversations

* patient listening

* consistent presence

The Power of Listening

Most adults listen to respond.

Few listen to understand.

When a child speaks, they are asking:

"Will you hear me… or correct me?"

The Listening Rule

When your child talks;

* Don't interrupt

* Don't rush to fix

* Don't dismiss

Instead,

Receive first. Respond later.

Case Study3: The Interrupted Child

"Daddy, today in school......."

"Wait, not now."

"Mommy, I want to tell you......."

"Later, I'm busy."

Over time, the child learns;

"My voice is not important."

And eventually…

The child stops discussing his/her matters with either of the parents.

What Silence Creates

When children don't speak:

* problems grow unseen

* mistakes go unshared

* emotions stay hidden

The Safe Space Principle

Your child must feel;

"I can tell you anything, even if it's wrong."

That does not mean:

No correction.

It means, *correction without fear*

How to Respond When a Child Tells the Truth

Instead of reacting with anger

Pause.

Then say,

"I'm glad you told me."

This builds;

✓ honesty

✓ trust

✓ openness

Communication Shapes Identity

The way you speak to your child becomes the way they speak to themselves

If they hear,

"You always mess up"

They believe: "I am careless."

If they hear;

"You can do better, I believe in you"

They believe: "I can improve."

Words Matter More Than You Think

They don't just correct behavior.

They shape,

* confidence

* self-image

* emotional strength

A Simple Daily Practice

Create a daily moment of connection:;

* during meals

* before bed

* while walking

Ask:

"What made you happy today?"

"Was anything difficult?"

Then listen.

Fully.

When Trust Is Strong

Something powerful happens.

You no longer need to:

* shout often

* repeat endlessly

* enforce harshly

Because your child begins to *listen willingly*

The Long-Term Impact

A child who trusts you will;

* come to you with problems

* listen to your guidance

* respect your voice

Not out of fear, but out of *connection*.

Final Truth

Discipline without communication creates distance.

But discipline with trust creates influence.

And influence is far more powerful than control.

The goal is to raise individuals who make responsible decisions independently.

Beyond Obedience

There is a question every parent must eventually face, and that is;

"What kind of adult will my child become?"

Not:

* Will they obey me?

* Will they behave at home?

But:

* Will they make good decisions when I am not there?

* Will they handle pressure?

* Will they take responsibility for their actions?

Because one day, there will be no supervision.

No reminders.

No correction in the moment.

And in that moment, your child will rely on;

what has been built inside him /her.

The Illusion of Control

Many parents believe;

"If I can control my child now, they will behave later."

But, control has a limit.

It only works when;

* you are present

* you are watching

* you are enforcing

Remove those…and what remains?

The Risk of Control-Based Parenting

A child raised only on control may become;

* dependent on authority
* unable to think independently
* obedient under pressure, but lost without it

 The Goal Is Internal Discipline

Not;

"Do this because I said so."

But;

"Do this because it is right."

Case Study 1: Two Different Outcomes

Two children.

Two homes.

Two approaches.

Child A

Raised with strict control.

Rules were clear.

Punishment was immediate.

Obedience was expected.

As a child:

✓ well-behaved

✓ quiet

✓ compliant

But as a teenager;

* started hiding things

* made poor decisions when unsupervised

* struggled with independence

Child B

Raised with guidance and structure.

Rules existed but, so did explanation.

Discipline was firm but, calm.

As a child:

✓ sometimes questioned

✓ sometimes resisted

But over time;

* developed judgment

* made thoughtful decisions

* took responsibility

The Difference

Child A learned:

"Follow instructions."

Child B learned:

"Understand and choose."

What Responsibility Really Means

Responsibility is not;

* blind obedience

* fear-based compliance

It is the ability to make the right choice, without supervision.

 How Responsibility Is Built

Not in one moment but, over time through;

* guidance

* consistency

* opportunity

Step 1: Give Age-Appropriate Responsibility

Children must practice responsibility.

Examples:

* packing their school bag

* cleaning their space

* managing small tasks

Not perfectly.

But consistently.

The Mistake Many Parents Make

Doing everything for the child.

This creates; dependence, not responsibility in the child.

Step 2: Allow Natural Consequences

If a child forgets something,

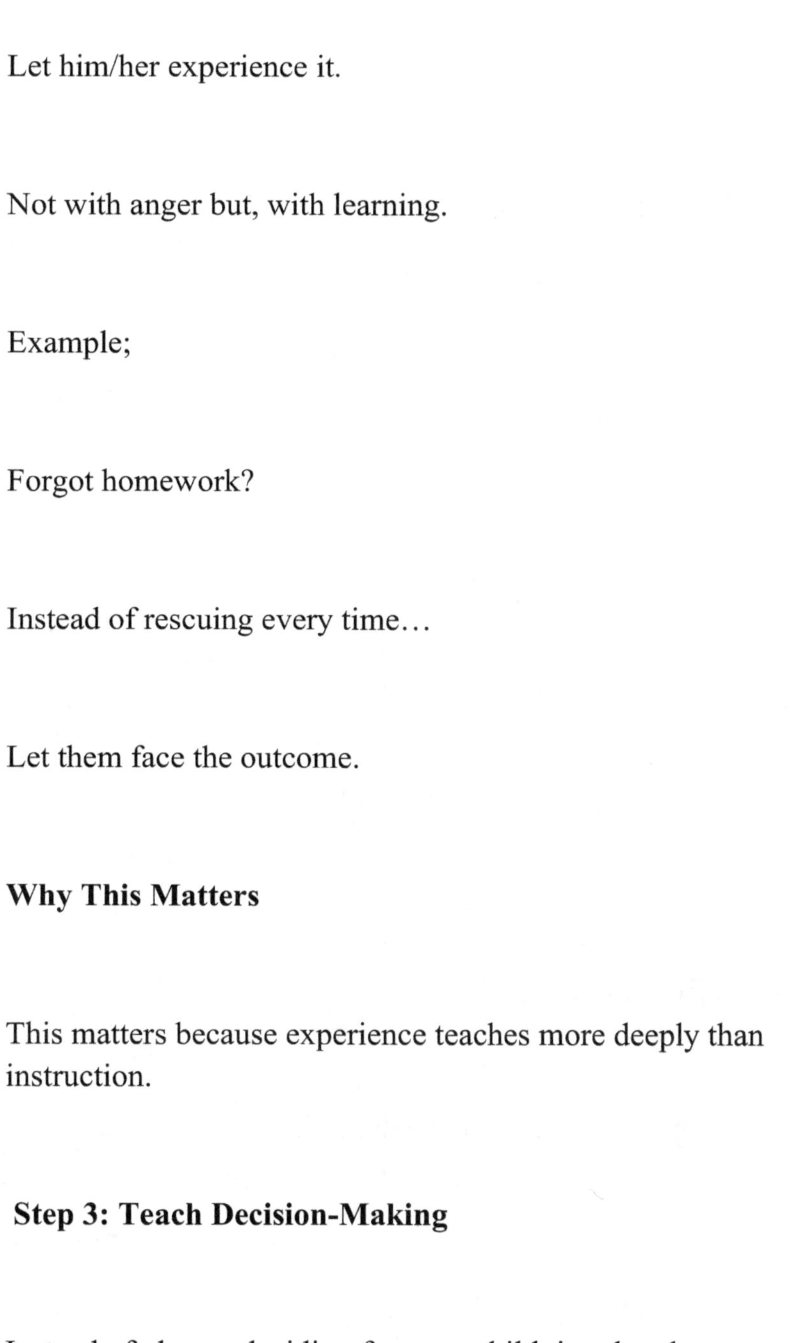

Let him/her experience it.

Not with anger but, with learning.

Example;

Forgot homework?

Instead of rescuing every time…

Let them face the outcome.

Why This Matters

This matters because experience teaches more deeply than instruction.

Step 3: Teach Decision-Making

Instead of always deciding for your child, involve them.

Ask;

* "What do you think is the right thing to do?"

* "What could happen if you choose this?"

This builds:

✓ thinking

✓ awareness

✓ judgment

Step 4: Model Responsibility

Children learn more from what you do than what you say.

If you;

* admit mistakes

* stay consistent

* act responsibly

They learn;

"this is how to live."

Case Study 2 : The Parent Who Apologized

One evening, a father shouted at his son unnecessarily.

Later, he returned.

"I was wrong to speak to you like that," he said.

"I'm sorry."

The boy looked surprised.

Then something changed.

What That Moment Taught

* accountability

* humility

* emotional strength

More powerful than any lecture.

A Hard Truth for Parents

You cannot teach responsibility, while avoiding it yourself.

Step 5: Build Accountability, Not Fear

When a child makes a mistake, instead of;

"Why did you do this?!"

Try;

"What happened?"

"How can we fix this?"

This builds;

✓ ownership

✓ problem-solving

✓ growth

The Long-Term Vision

You are not preparing your child for:

* childhood

* school

You are preparing him /her for life.

A life where they must:

* make decisions

* face consequences

* handle pressure

* navigate relationships

What Truly Successful Parenting Looks Like

Not raising;

✓ a quiet child

✓ a perfectly obedient child

But;

✓ a thinking adult

✓ a responsible adult

✓ a self-guided adult

A Powerful Reflection

Ask yourself:

"If I am not there will my child still do what is right?"

If the answer is:

* maybe

* sometimes

* I'm not sure

Then, the focus must shift.

Final Truth

You are not raising a child to follow you forever.

You are raising a person to;

stand, choose, and act on their own.

And that requires;

* guidance

* trust

* responsibility

Not fear. Not control. Neither punishment.

CONCLUSION: THE PARENT YOU ARE BECOMING

It Was Never Just About the Child

If you have read this far, something has already shifted.

Maybe quietly.

Maybe deeply.

But something has changed.

Because this book was never just about;

* stopping bad behavior

* correcting mistakes

* managing children

It was about something greater, which is;

Becoming the kind of parent who builds people, not just controls them.

The Journey You Have Begun

At the beginning, the focus may have been;

* "How do I make my child listen?"

* "How do I stop this behavior?"

* "How do I get things under control?"

But now, the questions are different.

Now you are asking;

* "What is my child learning from me?"

* "What kind of person am I raising?"

* "What kind of parent am I becoming?"

And that shift is everything.

The Truth About Change

Change in parenting does not happen overnight.

You will still have moments when;

* you lose patience

* your voice rises

* you react too quickly

That does not erase your progress.

It does not make you a failure. Rather,

It makes you human and growing.

What Matters Now

Not perfection but, awareness.

Not control but, intention.

Because every moment now holds a new possibility;

*To pause

*To choose differently

*To respond with purpose

The Child Is Learning Always

Even when you think nothing is happening, something is.

Your child is learning:

* how to respond to pressure

* how to handle mistakes

* how to treat others

* how to see themselves

Not from what you say.

But from how you show up.

The Parent as a Mirror

Children reflect what they experience.

If they experience,

* fear they learn fear

* shouting they learn shouting

* control they learn resistance

But if they experience:

* calm, they learn calm

* respect, they learn respect

* guidance, they learn responsibility

The Legacy You Are Building

One day, your child will grow up.

And when they do, they will carry something with them.

Not just:

* education

* achievements

* skills

But something deeper, which is the voice you helped create inside them.

Will that voice say:

* "I am afraid to fail"?

  Or

* "I can learn and grow"?

Will it say:

* "I must hide my mistakes"?

  Or

* "I can face them and improve"?

That voice is being built now and everyday.

When Discipline Becomes Something More

At the beginning, discipline may have felt like:

* correction

* control

* reaction

But now, you see it differently.

Now it becomes guidance.

It becomes a way to;

* teach

* shape

* strengthen

Not just behavior, but character.

The Power of Consistency

You do not need to be perfect. All you need to be;

consistent enough to create patterns

Patterns of;

* calm responses

* clear expectations

* respectful communication.

Over time, these patterns become habits.

And those habits become identity.

A Final Reflection

Pause for a moment.

Think about your child.

Not their behavior.

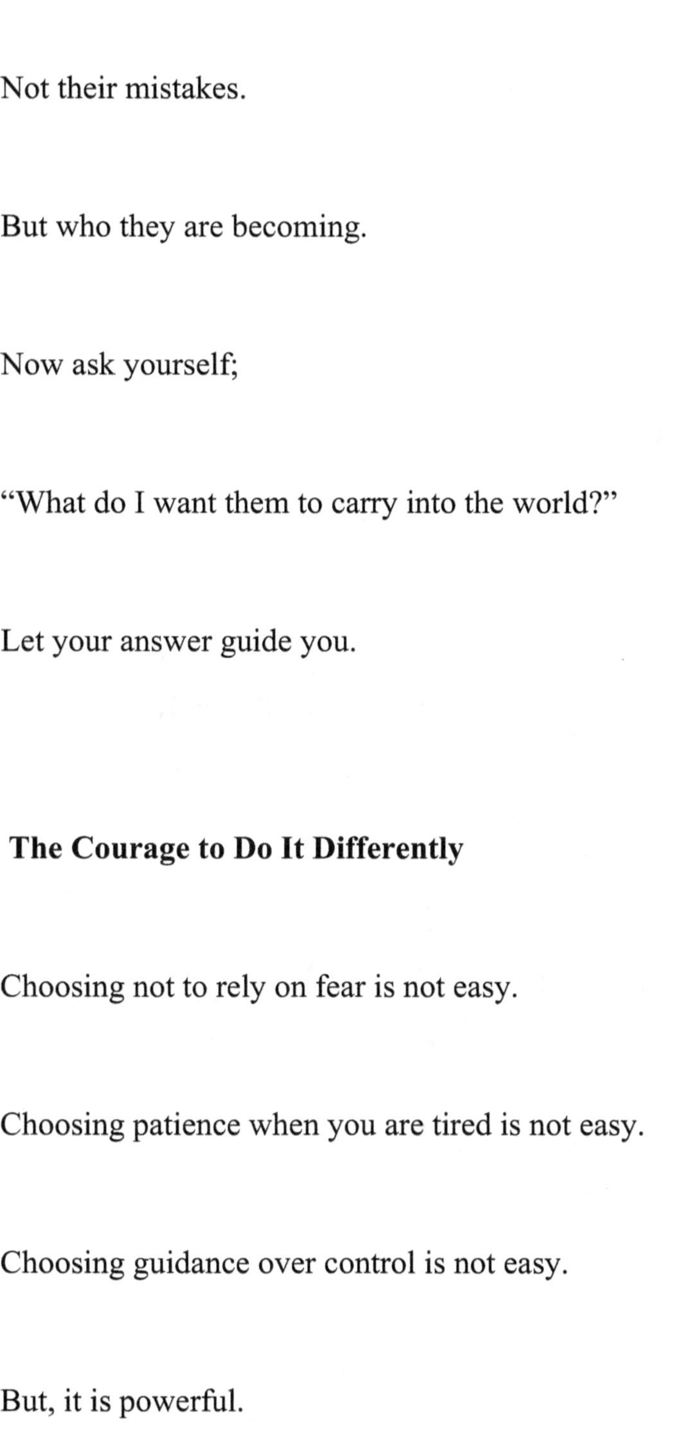

Not their mistakes.

But who they are becoming.

Now ask yourself;

"What do I want them to carry into the world?"

Let your answer guide you.

The Courage to Do It Differently

Choosing not to rely on fear is not easy.

Choosing patience when you are tired is not easy.

Choosing guidance over control is not easy.

But, it is powerful.

Because you are not just managing today.

You are shaping *a lifetime*.

A Message to You

You will have hard days.

You will have moments you wish you handled differently.

That is part of the journey.

But every time you choose to:

* pause instead of react

* listen instead of dismiss

* guide instead of punish

You are building something meaningful.

Final Words

You are not just raising a child.

You are raising:

* a thinker

* a decision-maker

* a human being with a voice, a mind, and a future

And you are not just parenting.

You are becoming*a guide, a teacher, a builder of lives*

The Last Truth

The goal is not a child who fears you.

The goal is not a child who simply obeys you.

The goal is a child who understands, chooses, and grows even when you are not there.

And that journey starts with you.